Passover

Passover

Winston Press

Winston Press, Inc.
600 First Avenue North
Minneapolis, MN 55403

The scripture quoted in this work is copyrighted by and
used through the courtesy of The Jewish Publication
Society of America.

Dieric Bouts (c. 1415-75)
The Gathering of the Manna (detail)
Church of St Pierre, Louvain, Belgium

Half-title: The Brother Haggadah
(Catalonia, late fourteenth century)
*The Plague of the Firstborn; The Israelites
Despoiling the Egyptians*
By permission of the British Library, London

Frontispiece: Pietro Perugino (c. 1445/50-1523) and
Bernadino di Betto Pintoricchio (c. 1454-1513)
The Journey of Moses into Egypt (detail)
Sistine Chapel, Vatican, Rome

Contents

Moses

AND there went a man of the house of Levi, and took to wife a daughter of Levi.

And the woman conceived, and bore a son: and when she saw him that he was a goodly child, she hid him three months.

And when she could not longer hide him, she took for him an ark of bulrushes, and daubed it with slime and with pitch; and she put the child therein, and laid it in the flags by the river's brink.

EXODUS 2·1-3

AND his sister stood afar off, to know what would be done to him.

And the daughter of Pharaoh came down to bathe in the river; and her maidens walked along by the river-side; and she saw the ark among the flags, and sent her maid to fetch it.

And she opened it, and saw it, even the child; and behold a boy that wept. And she had compassion on him, and said: 'This is one of the Hebrews' children.'

EXODUS 2·4-6

Paolo Veronese (c.1528-88)
Moses Rescued from the Water
Prado, Madrid

ND it came to pass in those days, when Moses was grown up, that he went out unto his brethren, and looked on their burdens; and he saw an Egyptian smiting a Hebrew, one of his brethren.

And he looked this way and that way, and when he saw that there was no man, he smote the Egyptian, and hid him in the sand.

EXODUS 2·11-12

Queen Mary Psalter (early fourteenth century)
An Episode from the Youth of Moses: Moses Slaying the Egyptian
By permission of the British Library, London

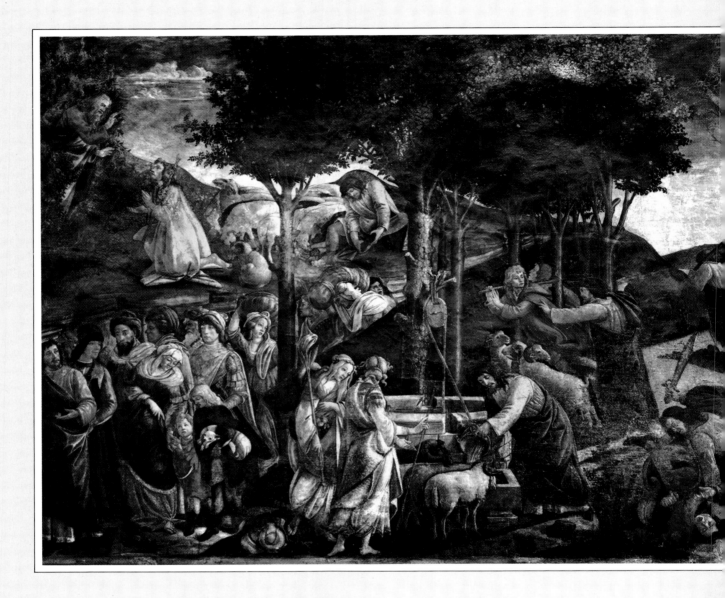

Sandro Botticelli (1445-1510)
Events in the Life of Moses
Sistine Chapel, Vatican, Rome

N OW the priest of Midian had seven daughters; and they came and drew water, and filled the troughs to water their fathers' flock.

And the shepherds came and drove them away; but Moses stood up and helped them, and watered their flock.

EXODUS 2·16-17

NOW Moses was keeping the flock of Jethro his father-in-law, the priest of Midian; and he led the flock to the farthest end of the wilderness, and came to the mountain of God, unto Horeb.

And the angel of the LORD appeared unto him in a flame of fire out of the midst of a bush; and he looked, and, behold, the bush burned with fire, and the bush was not consumed.

And Moses said: 'I will now turn aside now, and see this great sight, why the bush is not burnt.'

And when the LORD saw that he turned aside to see, God called unto him out of the midst of the bush, and said, 'Moses, Moses.'

And he said, 'Here am I.' And He said, 'Draw not nigh hither; put off thy shoes from off thy feet, for the place whereon thou standest is holy ground.'

EXODUS 3·1-5

The Golden Haggadah (Barcelona, c.1320)
*Moses before the Burning Bush; Moses Taking his Family back to Egypt and
Meeting Aaron; Moses and Aaron before Pharaoh*
By permission of the British Library, London

AND the LORD said: 'I have surely seen the affliction of My people that are in Egypt, and have heard their cry by reason of their taskmasters; for I know their pains.

And I am come down to deliver them out of the hand of the Egyptians, and to bring them up out of that land unto a good land and a large, unto a land flowing with milk and honey; . . .

And now, behold, the cry of the children of Israel is come unto Me; moreover I have seen the oppression wherewith the Egyptians oppress them.

Come now therefore, and I will send thee unto Pharaoh, that thou mayest bring forth My people the children of Israel out of Egypt.

EXODUS 3·7-10

The Barcelona Haggadah (Barcelona, mid-fourteenth century)
'We were slaves unto Pharaoh in Egypt and were taken out by the strong arm of God'
By permission of the British Library, London

עבדים

היינו

לפרעה במצרים ויוצאנו

יי אלהינו משם ביד חזקה

ובזרוע נטויה ולא הוציא

AND Moses said unto God: 'Who am I, that I should go unto Pharaoh, and that I should bring forth the children of Israel out of Egypt?'

And He said: 'Certainly I will be with thee; and this shall be the token unto thee, that I have sent thee: When thou hast brought forth the people out of Egypt, ye shall serve God upon this mountain.'

EXODUS 3·11-12

AND Moses answered and said: 'But, behold, they will not believe me, nor hearken unto my voice; for they will say: The LORD hath not appeared unto thee.'

And the LORD said unto him: 'What is that in thine hand?' And he said: 'A rod.'

And He said: 'Cast it on the ground.' And he cast it on the ground, and it became a serpent; and Moses fled from before it.

EXODUS 4·1-3

The Rylands Haggadah (Catalonia, mid-fourteenth century)
Moses before the Burning Bush; 'What is there in thy hand?'
The John Rylands University Library, Manchester

Pietro Perugino (c.1445/50-1523)
and Bernadino di Betto Pintoricchio (1454-1513)
The Journey of Moses into Egypt
Sistine Chapel, Vatican, Rome

AND the LORD said unto Moses in Midian: 'Go, return into Egypt; for all the men are dead that sought thy life.'

And Moses took his wife and his sons, and set them upon an ass, and he returned to the land of Egypt; and Moses took the rod of God in his hand.

EXODUS 4·19-20

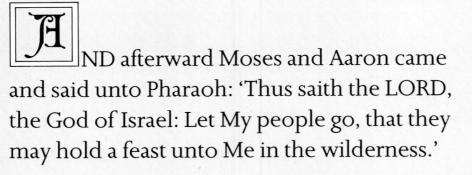ND the LORD said to Aaron: 'Go into the wilderness to meet Moses.' And he went, and met him in the mountain of God, and kissed him.

And Moses told Aaron all the words of the LORD wherewith He had sent him, and all the signs wherewith He had charged him.

EXODUS 4·27-28

ND afterward Moses and Aaron came and said unto Pharaoh: 'Thus saith the LORD, the God of Israel: Let My people go, that they may hold a feast unto Me in the wilderness.'

And Pharaoh said: 'Who is the LORD, that I should hearken unto his voice to let Israel go? I know not the LORD, and moreover I will not let Israel go.'

EXODUS 5·1-2

The Rylands Haggadah (Catalonia, mid-fourteenth century)
Moses and Aaron before Pharaoh; The Labour of the Israelites
The John Rylands University Library, Manchester

The Plagues

ND the LORD said unto Moses: 'Now shalt thou see what I will do to Pharaoh; for by a strong hand shall he let them go, and by a strong hand shall he drive them out of his land.'

And God spoke unto Moses, and said unto him: 'I am the LORD;'

EXODUS 6.1-2

THUS saith the LORD: In this thou shalt know that I am the LORD — behold, I will smite with the rod that is in my hand upon the waters which are in the river, and they shall be turned to blood.

And the fish that are in the river shall die, and the river shall become foul; and the Egyptians shall loathe to drink water from the river.

EXODUS 7·17-18

The Brother Haggadah (Catalonia, late fourteenth century)
Aaron's Rod Swallowing the Magicians' Rods; The Plague of Blood
By permission of the British Library, London

AND the LORD spoke unto Moses: 'Go in unto Pharaoh, and say unto him: Thus saith the LORD: Let my people go, that they may serve me.

And if thou refuse to let them go, behold, I will smite all thy borders with frogs.

And the river shall swarm with frogs, which shall go up and come into thy house, and into thy bedchamber, and upon thy bed, and into the house of thy servants, and upon thy people, and into thine ovens, and into thy kneadingtroughs.'

EXODUS 7·26-28

NOW therefore send, hasten in thy cattle and all that thou hast in the field; for every man and beast that shall be found in the field, and shall not be brought home, the hail shall come down upon them, and they shall die.

EXODUS 9·19

The Golden Haggadah (Barcelona, c.1320)
*The Plague of Frogs; The Plague of Lice; The Plague of 'Arov;
The Plague of Murrain*
By permission of the British Library, London

27

BEHOLD, the hand of the LORD is upon thy cattle which are in the field, upon the horses, upon the asses, upon the camels, upon the herds, and upon the flocks; there shall be a very grievous murrain.

EXODUS 9·3

AND the LORD did that thing on the morrow, and all the cattle of Egypt died; but of the cattle of the children of Israel died not one.

EXODUS 9·6

The Brother Haggadah (Catalonia, late fourteenth century)
The Plague of 'Arov; The Plague of Murrain
By permission of the British Library, London

ND the LORD said unto Moses and unto Aaron: 'Take to you handfuls of soot of the furnace, and let Moses throw it heavenward in the sight of Pharaoh.

And it shall become small dust over all the land of Egypt, and shall be a boil breaking forth with blains upon man and upon beast, throughout all the land of Egypt.'

And they took soot of the furnace, and stood before Pharaoh; and Moses threw it up heavenward; and it became a boil breaking forth with blains upon man, and upon beast.

EXODUS 9·8-10

The Brother Haggadah (Catalonia, late fourteenth century)
The Plague of Boils; The Plague of Hail
By permission of the British Library, London

31

ELSE, if thou refuse to let My people go, behold, to-morrow will I bring locusts into thy border;

and they shall cover the face of the earth, that one shall not be able to see the earth: and they shall eat the residue of that which is escaped, which remaineth unto you from the hail, and shall eat every tree which groweth for you out of the field;

EXODUS 10·4-5

AND the LORD said unto Moses: 'Stretch out thy hand toward heaven, that there may be darkness over the land of Egypt, even darkness which may be felt.'

And Moses stretched forth his hand toward heaven; and there was a thick darkness in all the land of Egypt three days;

EXODUS 10·21-22

The Brother Haggadah (Catalonia, late fourteenth century)
The Plague of Locusts; The Plague of Darkness
By permission of the British Library, London

The Passover

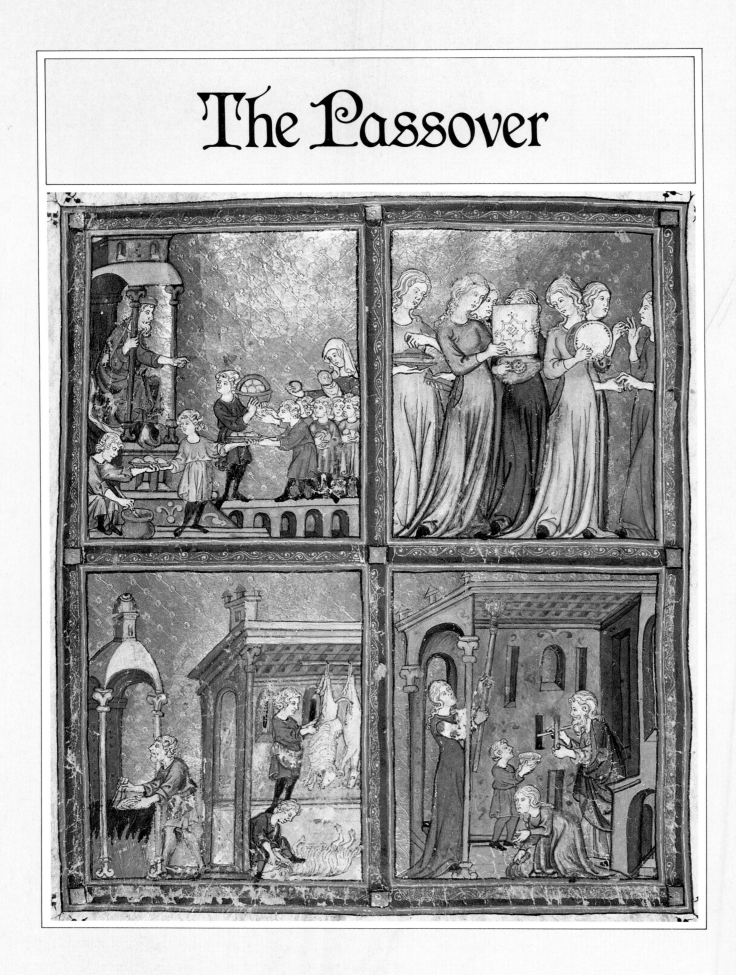

THEN Moses called for all the elders of Israel, and said unto them: 'Draw out, and take you lambs according to your families, and kill the passover lamb.

And ye shall take a bunch of hyssop, and dip it in the blood that is in the basin, and strike the lintel and the two side-posts with the blood that is in the basin; and none of you shall go out of the door of his house until the morning.

For the LORD will pass through to smite the Egyptians; and when He seeth the blood upon the lintel, and on the two side-posts, the LORD will pass over the door, and will not suffer the destroyer to come in unto your houses to smite you.

And ye shall observe this thing for an ordinance to thee and to thy sons for ever.'

EXODUS 12·21-24

The Golden Haggadah (Barcelona, c.1320)
Miriam and Her Maidens Play, Sing and Dance; Distribution of Mazzot and Haroset; Preparing the Paschal Lamb and Cleansing Dishes; Searching for Leaven
By permission of the British Library, London

ND it came to pass at midnight, that the LORD smote all the firstborn in the land of Egypt, from the firstborn of Pharaoh that sat on his throne unto the firstborn of the captive that was in the dungeon; and all the firstborn of cattle.

And Pharaoh rose up in the night, he, and all his servants, and all the Egyptians; and there was a great cry in Egypt; for there was not a house where there was not one dead.

And he called for Moses and Aaron by night and said: 'Rise up, get you forth from among my people, both ye and the children of Israel; and go, serve the LORD, as ye have said.

Take both your flocks and your herds, as ye have said, and be gone; and bless me also.'

And the Egyptians were urgent upon the people, to send them out of the land in haste; for they said: 'We are all dead men.'

EXODUS 12·29-33

Bernadino Luini (c.1485-1532)
The Slaying of the Firstborn
Pinacoteca di Brera, Milan

The Exodus

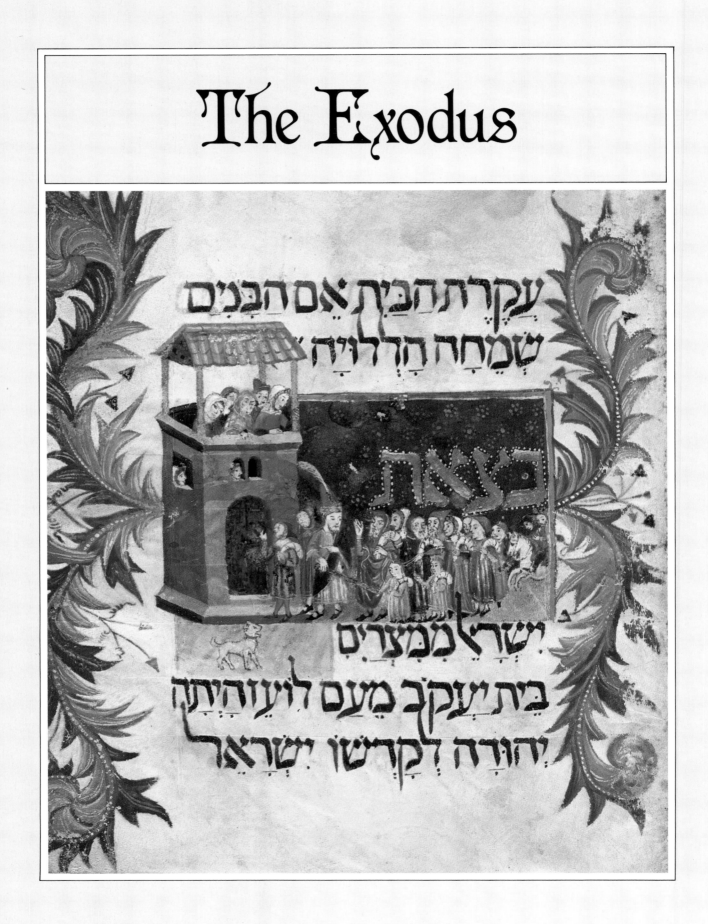

ND it came to pass, when Pharaoh had let the people go, that God led them not by the way of the land of the Philistines, although that was near; for God said: 'Lest peradventure the people repent when they see war, and they return to Egypt.'

But God led the people about, by the way of the wilderness of the Red Sea; and the children of Israel went up armed out of the land of Egypt.

EXODUS 13·17-18

ND the LORD went before them by day in a pillar of a cloud, to lead them the way; and by night in a pillar of fire, to give them light; that they might go by day and by night:

the pillar of cloud by day, and the pillar of fire by night, departed not from before the people.

EXODUS 13·21-22

Kaufmann Haggadah (Spain, fourteenth century)
Moses leading the Children of Israel out of the City Gate
Library of Hungarian Academy of Sciences, Budapest

AND the Egyptians pursued after them, all the horses and chariots of Pharaoh, and his horsemen, and his army, and overtook them encamping by the sea, beside Pi-hahiroth, in front of Baal-zephon.

And when Pharaoh drew nigh, the children of Israel lifted up their eyes, and, behold, the Egyptians were marching after them; and they were sore afraid; and the children of Israel cried out unto the LORD.

EXODUS 14·9-10

The Brother Haggadah (Catalonia, late fourteenth century)
The Israelites Leaving Egypt; The Pursuing Egyptians
By permission of the British Library, London

41

Lucas Cranach the Elder (1472-1553)
The Submersion of Pharaoh's Army
Alte Pinakothek, Munich

AND Moses stretched forth his hand over the sea, and the sea returned to its strength when the morning appeared; and the Egyptians fled against it; and the LORD overthrew the Egyptians in the midst of the sea.

And the waters returned, and covered the chariots, and the horsemen, even all the host of Pharaoh that went in after them into the sea; there remained not so much as one of them.

But the children of Israel walked upon dry land in the midst of the sea; and the waters were a wall unto them on their right hand, and on their left.

EXODUS 14·27-29

Manna

Giuseppe Angeli (1709-98)
The Falling of the Manna
Church of San Stae, Venice

ND they took their journey from Elim, and all the congregation of the children of Israel came unto the wilderness of Sin, which is between Elim and Sinai, on the fifteenth day of the second month after their departing out of the land of Egypt.

And the whole congregation of the children of Israel murmured against Moses and against Aaron in the wilderness;

and the children of Israel said unto them: 'Would that we had died by the hand of the LORD in the land of Egypt, when we sat by the flesh pots; when we did eat bread to the full; for ye have brought us forth into this wilderness, to kill this whole assembly with hunger.'

Then said the LORD unto Moses: 'Behold, I will rain bread from heaven for you; and the people shall go out and gather a day's portion every day, that I may prove them, whether they will walk in My law, or not.'

And it shall come to pass on the sixth day that they shall prepare that which they bring in, and it shall be twice as much as they gather daily.

EXODUS 16·1-5

AND when the children of Israel saw it, they said one to another: 'What is it' — for they knew not what it was. And Moses said unto them: 'It is the bread which the LORD hath given you to eat.

This is the thing which the LORD hath commanded: Gather ye of it every man according to his eating, an omer a head, according to the number of your persons, shall ye take it, every man for them that are in his tent.'

And the children of Israel did so, and gathered some more, some less.

EXODUS 16·15-17

Bacchiacca (1495-1557)
The Gathering of the Manna
National Gallery, Washington (Samuel H. Kress Collection)

The Covenant

ND the LORD said unto Moses: 'Come up to Me into the mount and be there; and I will give thee the tables of stone, and the law and commandment, which I have written, that thou mayest teach them.

And Moses rose up, and Joshua his minister; and Moses went up into the mount of God.

And unto the elders he said: 'Tarry ye here for us, until we come back unto you: and, behold, Aaron and Hur are with you; whosoever hath a cause, let him come unto them.'

And Moses went up into the mount, and the cloud covered the mount.

EXODUS 24·12-15

Guido Reni (1575-1642)
Moses with the Tablets of the Law
Galleria Borghese, Rome

AND Moses entered into the midst of the cloud, and went up into the mount: and Moses was in the mount forty days and forty nights.

EXODUS 24·18

Justus of Ghent (Joos van Wassenhove) (active c. 1460-80)
Moses with the Tablets of the Law
Palazzo Ducale, Urbino

AND the LORD spoke unto Moses: 'Go, get thee down; for thy people, that thou broughtest up out of the land of Egypt, have dealt corruptly;

they have turned aside quickly out of the way which I commanded them; they have made them a molten calf, and have worshipped it, and have sacrificed unto it, and said: 'This is thy god, O Israel, which have brought thee up out of the land of Egypt.'

EXODUS 32·7-8

Nicolas Poussin (1594-1665)
The Worship of the Golden Calf
National Gallery, London

AND it came to pass, as soon as he came nigh unto the camp, that he saw the calf, and the dancing; and Moses' anger waxed hot, and he cast the tables out of his hands, and broke them beneath the mount.

EXODUS 32·19

Rembrandt Harmensz van Rijn (1606-69)
Moses Breaking the Tables of the Law
Staatliche Museen, West Berlin

AND the LORD said unto Moses: 'Make thee a fiery serpent, and set it upon a pole; and it shall come to pass, that every one that is bitten, when he seeth it, shall live.

And Moses made a serpent of brass, and set it upon the pole; and it came to pass, that if a serpent had bitten any man, when he looked unto the serpent of brass, he lived.

NUMBERS 21·8-9

Peter Paul Rubens (1577-1640) and
Anthony van Dyck (1599-1641)
The Brazen Serpent
Prado, Madrid

The Promised Land

AND Moses went up from the plains of Moab unto mount Nebo, to the top of Pisgah, that is over against Jericho. And the LORD showed him all the land, even Gilead as far as Dan;

and all Naphtali, and the land of Ephraim and Manasseh, and all the land of Judah, as far as the hinder sea;

and the South, and the Plain, even the valley of Jericho, the city of palm-trees, as far as Zoar.

And the LORD said unto him: 'This is the land which I swore unto Abraham, unto Isaac, and unto Jacob, saying: I will give it unto thy seed; I have caused thee to see it with thine eyes, but thou shalt not go over thither.'

DEUTERONOMY 34·1-4

Luca Signorelli (1441?-1523)
The Testament and Death of Moses (detail)
Sistine Chapel, Vatican, Rome

SO Moses the servant of the LORD died there in the land of Moab, according to the word of the LORD.

And he was buried in the valley in the land of Moab over against Beth-peor; and no man knoweth of his sepulchre unto this day.

And Moses was a hundred and twenty years old when he died: his eye was not dim, nor his natural force abated.

DEUTERONOMY 34·5-7

Luca Signorelli (1441?-1523)
The Testament and Death of Moses (detail)
Sistine Chapel, Vatican, Rome

AND the children of Israel wept for Moses in the plains of Moab thirty days; so the days of weeping in the mourning for Moses were ended.

And Joshua the son of Nun was full of the spirit of wisdom; for Moses had laid his hands upon him; and the children of Israel hearkened unto him, and did as the Lord commanded Moses.

And there hath not arisen a prophet since in Israel like unto Moses, whom the LORD knew face to face;

in all the signs and the wonders, which the LORD sent him to do in the land of Egypt, to Pharaoh, and to all his servants, and to all his land;

and in all the mighty hand, and in all the great terror, which Moses wrought in the sight of all Israel.

DEUTERONOMY 34·8-12

ACKNOWLEDGEMENTS

The Publishers are grateful to the museums, galleries and
collections to which the paintings belong, as well as Archivio
I.G.D.A., Corvina Archives, Budapest (Alfréd Schiller), and Scala
for their kind permission to reproduce illustrations in this book.